# ALICE WATERS *and the* TRIP TO DELICIOUS

WRITTEN BY **JACQUELINE BRIGGS MARTIN**

ILLUSTRATED BY **HAYELIN CHOI**

**AFTERWORD BY ALICE WATERS**

Readers *to* Eaters

BELLEVUE, WASHINGTON

READERS to EATERS
12437 SE 26th Place, Bellevue, WA 98005
**ReadersToEaters.com**

Distributed by Publishers Group West


Printed in the U.S.A. by Worzalla, Stevens Point, Wisconsin (4/14)

Book Design by Red Herring Design
Book production by The Kids at Our House

Photograph of Alice Waters on page 31 by David Liittschwager.

The art is done in brush and black ink, scanned digitally, then colored and each element combined using Adobe Photoshop.

The text is set in Cochin and Neutraface. Cochin is a transitional serif font based on the copperplate engravings of French artist Nicholas Cochin, and was originally produced in 1912 by Georges Peignot for the Parisian foundry Deberny & Peignot. Neutraface is a sans-serif typeface designed by Christian Schwartz for the American type foundry, House Industries. It's geometric forms reference modernist architect Richard Neutra's design principles and signage used on his buildings.

10 9 8 7 6 5 4 3 2 1
First Edition

Library of Congress Control Number: 2014939601
ISBN 978-0983661566

# DEDICATION

To my mother, Alice Briggs.
Like Alice Waters, she knows that delicious food and good times go together.
**—J.B.M.**

To my mom and dad, who taught me there are so many delicious foods around the world. **—H.C.**

Some people want new red shoes.
Some want to sing on stage
or play basketball.

Chef Alice Waters wants every kid in the country
to come with her on the trip to Delicious.

She wants
the hungry kids, the happy kids,
the tall kids, the short kids
to have a delicious lunch—every day.
She wants them to know the taste of good food,
know the story of food.
Every kid—millions of kids!
Where did Alice Waters
get such an idea?

Well, Alice Waters has always
been friends with food.

When she was three years old,
she wore food—
a lettuce-leaf skirt, radish bracelets,
a necklace of strawberries, a crown of asparagus—
and won first prize in a costume contest.

Little Alice was also looking for Delicious.
And she found it in
fresh green beans, sweet corn,
and just-picked blueberries.

**ALICE WAS ALWAYS VERY AWARE OF SMELLS AND FLAVORS.** As a child, she loved applesauce, grilled steak, and strawberries, but not bananas or dry brown bread.

1

When she was in college, Alice went to France
and studied food (not books).
She walked the markets,
tasting savory onion soup,
buying sweet carrots, warm bread, sausages.
She and her French friends
spent hours cooking,
eating, talking, and laughing.

In her travels, Alice learned
wonderful food was like a symphony
that woke people up, made them happier.
Sharing good food
could start a party, make memories.

**ONCE IN TURKEY, A BOY HAD SHARED TEA AND HIS LAST BITS OF CHEESE WITH ALICE AND HER FRIENDS.** She said that kindness changed her life.

Back home, Alice wanted to take her American friends
on the trip to Delicious.
She wanted them to have the meals and the good times
she had loved in France.
She searched long hours for fresh vegetables,
fish, meat, and herbs.

She simmered stews, roasted chickens, baked tarts.
Her friends filled Alice's place
and stayed for hours enjoying the amazing dinners.
People who ate Alice's meals called her a "genius" with food,
but her home wasn't big enough for all her friends.

CHEZ:PANISSE

Alice started to dream of a new kind of restaurant
with wonderful food and helpful waiters,
a small restaurant that welcomed people
to eat, sit, and visit.

Alice found a place,
fixed it up with her friends,
and named it after Panisse,
a kindly character from a French movie.

Chez Panisse ("Panisse's House")
was like a house, a home
where the staff—chefs to dishwashers—worked together,
laughed together, and ate together.
That first night they had such a crowd
they ran out of food.

And that was a problem—
finding enough fresh, tasty food.
Frozen food was handy.
Food that had been on the shelves for days
was cheap.
But those were not right for the trip to Delicious.
Alice worked day and night finding just the right food.
She drove to the fish and poultry markets
in Chinatown—so often that her car began to smell
like a fish wagon and no one wanted to ride with her.

**ALICE COULD NEVER RESIST SHARING DELICIOUS FOOD.**
Once she was carrying fresh strawberries on an airplane. Everyone on the plane could smell them. One by one they asked to taste a berry. By the time the plane landed, Alice was out of berries.

Alice and her friends picked wild fennel
beside railroad tracks;
knocked on strangers' doors and asked to pick
mulberries from their trees.
She planted lettuce in her own yard.

As news of Chez Panisse spread,
growers brought baskets
of their best vegetables to the back door.
Alice noticed that these plump, fresh vegetables
had the richest flavor.

**ALICE ALSO VISITED FARMS.** She walked the fields with farmers, tasting just-picked carrots or radishes, sometimes even a bit of soil.

She began to pay foragers to go out into the country
to find others who took good care of the earth,
their crops, and their animals.

The delicious meals she wanted to serve
to her customers
began not in the kitchen but in the field,
with good soil and thoughtful farmers.

Once she found the ingredients,
Alice tasted every dish the chefs cooked.
Maybe it needed a bit of onion,
an extra squeeze of lemon.
She wanted every meal to be a symphony of flavor.
If it did not taste just right to Alice, it couldn't be served.

Alice Waters and the Chez Panisse family
have cooked for a U.S. president
and a prince—even the Dalai Lama.
Alice was the first woman to win the James Beard Award
for "Outstanding Chef of the Year."

**"TASTING JUST RIGHT" DOES NOT ALWAYS MEAN FANCY FOOD.**
Alice says a carefully fried fresh egg or a ripe melon can be plenty for a party.

Alice cooked for kids, too.
At the restaurant they made a special kids' "dipping salad"
with a little lettuce heart, carrot curls,
and a bowl of oil and vinegar.

Alice made school lunch for her daughter, Fanny—
leafy greens, garlic toast, a piece of last night's chicken—
some tasty surprise to make her smile.

As she planned Fanny's lunches,
she wondered about other kids:
were they eating lunch? A good lunch?

Every day, walking from her home to Chez Panisse,
Alice passed a school with no kitchen,
just a hut at the edge of the parking lot,
where students could buy packaged foods, tired flavors.

Alice wanted those students
to eat meals that would make them smile,
that would make a party.
She wanted to take those schoolkids on the trip to Delicious.

She came up with an idea.
Students could grow their own food!
They would taste fresh green peas,
red tomatoes, kale, carrots, ripe apples.

To introduce the Edible Schoolyard idea to parents and students, Alice and the Chez Panisse staff invited them to a special taco dinner at the school. The dinner was a huge success. Students had so much fun flattening masa dough into tortillas they didn't want to quit.

It took two years to remove the pavement
and get the soil ready.
Then they planted.
Teachers and students went to the garden
to study the science of soil,
the math of spacing seeds in a row,
and the histories of vegetables.

Schoolkids
learned to cook the vegetables
in a kitchen classroom.
They learned to make eating a special time
with colorful plates, tablecloths.
Lunch with Alice tasted good!

This is what Alice Waters knows:
fresh food, grown in healthy soil,
brings us joy—the same joy
we get from a beautiful song
or a starry sky.
And every kid deserves that joy.

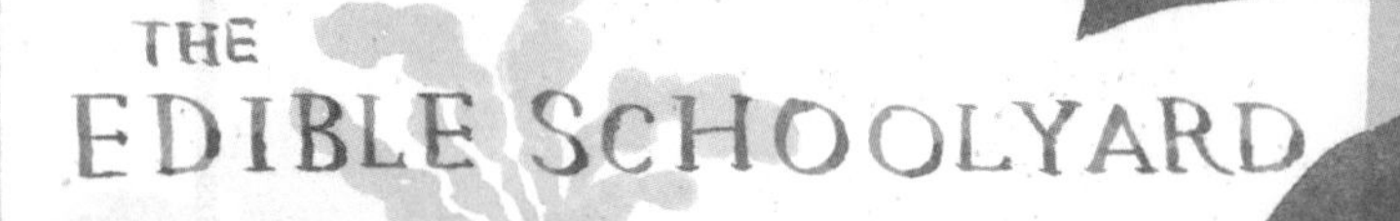

Alice travels thousands of miles
to help grow more Edible Schoolyards,
to spread the word about the vegetable symphony.

Because Alice Waters is sure:
kids who know good food,
who grow, gather, and share good food,
will care about the soil, care about farmers,
care about everyone having enough to eat.

Kids who get to Delicious can change the world.

# AFTERWORD

Dear Reader and Eater,

I hope you have liked hearing my story! Here are some things I have learned about food and cooking from my time at Chez Panisse and the Edible Schoolyard—and from my daughter, Fanny:

1) **GROW YOUR OWN FOOD.**
If you grow it and cook it yourself, you're going to want to eat it—even kale!

2) **TASTE AND TASTE AGAIN.**
Who knows what you are going to like? Always have a taste of everything—and remember that ripeness is all! You never forget the taste of a perfectly ripe peach.

3) **ALWAYS EAT IN SEASON.** I promise you that those supermarket tomatoes in the middle of winter are not going to taste good! You don't want to eat the same second-rate foods all year-round that aren't delicious—you want to wait for the juicy tomatoes and sweet corn in the heat of summer. They will be all the better for your wait.

4) **IF YOUR PLATE IS TOO FULL, IT IS HARD TO TASTE.** If something is truly delicious, you don't need to eat so much to be satisfied. It's when things don't have flavor that you eat more and more and more, searching for flavor that isn't there.

5) **COOK WITH YOUR FRIENDS!** You can talk about things when you're shelling fresh peas or washing lettuce, and you will have so much fun making food together. When you come together at the table and share a meal, you never know what you are going to learn.

I can't wait to see you all in the garden and the kitchen!

With hopefulness,

Alice Waters

ALICE WATERS

# AUTHOR'S *Note*

Alice Waters' dedication to finding the freshest, tastiest food for the customers at Chez Panisse has changed the way we think about food in America. Her commitment to giving everyone, especially kids, the experience of eating and sharing delicious food has reminded all of us that our sense of taste can give us as much pleasure as our senses of sight or hearing. Perfect peaches can make a party!

Because of Alice Waters and the Edible Schoolyard Project (started in 1995), thousands of students are growing food in schoolyard gardens and learning to make delicious meals in school kitchens. There are Edible Schoolyard gardens all over America and in twenty-nine other countries. And the program is still growing.

Restaurants have changed, too, because of Alice Waters. When Chez Panisse opened its doors in 1971, most chefs were men, and most cooks thought about finding the best recipes, not the best ingredients. Thanks to Chez Panisse, chefs all over America now search for locally grown, flavorful food, and list—on the menu or on the wall—the names of the farmers who grow the food they serve.

I hope readers of all ages will learn of Alice Waters and wonder about how to be part of the trip to Delicious—maybe grow lettuce in a bucket, or peppers in a plant pot, go to a farmers' market and find a red tomato, make a salad, fold a sandwich, and share it with a friend.

—Jacqueline Briggs Martin

## BIBLIOGRAPHY


Chez Panisse—*chezpanisse.com*

Curtan, Patricia. *Menus for Chez Panisse*. New York: Princeton Architectural Press, 2011.

McNamee, Thomas. *Alice Waters and Chez Panisse*. New York: Penguin, 2007.

Reichl, Ruth. "There Is Only One Chez Panisse." In *American Greats*, edited by Robert A. Wilson and Stanley Marcus, 40-43. New York: PublicAffairs, 1999.

Waters, Alice. *The Art of Simple Food: Notes, Lessons, and Recipes from a Delicious Revolution*. With Patricia Curtan, Kelsie Kerr & Fritz Streif. New York: Clarkson Potter, 2007.

——. *The Art of Simple Food II: Recipes, Flavor, and Inspiration From the New Kitchen Garden*. With Kelsie Kerr & Patricia Curtan. New York: Clarkson Potter, 2013.

——. *The Chez Panisse Menu Cookbook*. In collaboration with Linda P. Guenzel. New York: Random House, 1982.

——. *Edible Schoolyard: A Universal Idea*. San Francisco: Chronicle Books, 2008.

——. *Forty Years of Chez Panisse: The Power of Gathering*. New York: Clarkson Potter, 2011.


## RESOURCES

**FOR FURTHER READING AND GARDENING AND COOKING**

### GROW YOUR OWN:

***Good Reads related to growing your own food***

The Edible Schoolyard Project—*edibleschoolyard.org*

Slow Food USA National School Garden Project—*slowfoodusa.org/children-food*

Bartholomew, Mel. *Square Foot Gardening with Kids*. Minneapolis, MN: Cool Springs Press, 2014.

Bucklin-Sporer, Arden and Rachel Kathleen Pringle. *How to Grow a School Garden: A Complete Guide for Parents and Teachers*. Portland, OR: Timber Press, 2010.

Martin, Jacqueline Briggs. *Farmer Will Allen and the Growing Table*. Bellevue, WA: Readers to Eaters, 2013.

Pryor, Katherine. *Sylvia's Spinach*. Bellevue, WA: Readers to Eaters, 2012.

Swann, Rick. *Our School Garden!* Bellevue, WA: Readers to Eaters, 2012.

### COOK YOUR OWN:

***Good Reads that help you cook wonderful food***

ChopChop Families cooking—*chopchopmag.org*

Katzen, Mollie. *Honest Pretzels And 64 Other Amazing Recipes for Cooks Ages 8 and Up*. Berkeley, CA: Tricycle Press, 1999.

—— and Ann Henderson. *Pretend Soup and Other Real Recipes: A Cookbook for Preschoolers and Up*. Berkeley, CA: Tricycle Press, 1994.

Sampson, Sally. *ChopChop: The Kids' Guide to Cooking Real Food with Your Family*. New York: Simon & Schuster, 2013.

Waters, Alice. *Fanny at Chez Panisse: A Child's Restaurant Adventures with 46 Recipes*. With Bob Carrau and Patricia Curtan. New York: HarperPerennial, 1997.


**JACQUELINE BRIGGS MARTIN** is the author of numerous children's books, including *Snowflake Bentley*, winner of the Caldecott Medal. Her last book, *Farmer Will Allen and the Growing Table*, published by Readers to Eaters, was named an American Library Association Notable Book and was among the "Best Nonfiction Books 2013" by *School Library Journal*. She grew up on a farm in Maine and now lives in Mt. Vernon, Iowa. Learn more about Jacqueline at *jacquelinebriggsmartin.com*.

**HAYELIN CHOI** is an illustrator and textile designer. This is her first picture book. A native of Korea, she is a graduate of School of Visual Arts and lives in Queens, New York. Learn more about Hayelin at *hayelinchoi.com*.